INSPIRED
—— BY ——
THE HOLY GHOST

Spiritual Poetic Messages Received
from Popular Songs

VOLUME 1

AIMEE CABO NIKOLOV

ISBN: 9781736797402

Printed in the United States of America

Inspirational Books Publishing 18320 Franjo Road
Palmetto Bay FL 33157

Contents

PREFACE

I always found music therapeutic and discovered great meaning from songs. So, I wanted to share music in my radio talk show, The Cure. As I grew in my relationship with God these meanings started to form into poetic messages that would follow the one minute of the song that was played on the radio show. The same song can give different messages according to the atmosphere, my feeling and what was needed at the moment. It would follow the same idea from the one-minute clip of the song that was played as well as a key word, phrase or name of the song included to tie it together.

As a rule, I regularly asked the holy spirit for assistance in remembering what I originally thought when I first heard a particular song and would expand as necessary with what came to mind. To my surprise these poems I wrote from popular songs where of great help to me. After seeing how others appreciated them when they were posted, we decided to make it more available, in the hopes that they can comfort more people by including them in a book. if the holy spirit helped me, then it can help others.

May God bless all those who read it.

Yours truly,

Aimee

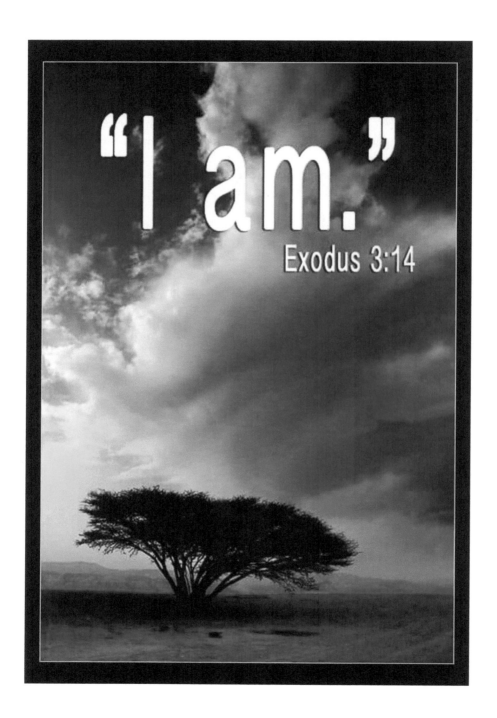

122, #4: "Amen" by King and Country

Some of us believe we came to existence
as a mere coincidence or by chance.

But who else would walk this world? Sacrificing his life,
creating miracles and for ages becoming our greatest romance.

It's the greatest amen that ever lived or can ever be.
It's our true inspiration, the fire that's breathing within us for everyone to see.

The world knows of him,
there is no one greater.
He imprinted his love in his children.
We are the product of such an awesome creator.

Amen, to his ultimate wisdom
that will guide us and carry us through
the challenges in life we may face.
Knowing his love is forever and his promises come true. 😌 🖤 🙏

From Aimee Cabo's *The Cure Radio Show* episode 122
"Diving into the Subconscious" #GodisTheCure

Inspired by the song "Amen" by King and Country
Full video podcast: http://apple.co/2M5g2dS

1

122, #3: "Goodbye" by Shaylen

Even the strongest among us
can struggle, slip up and fall.
No need to be discouraged,
We must be patient with ourselves,
it can be a long haul.

Though we are lost without God,
saying goodbye seems ok, but we choke.
The path may be difficult and narrow,
but keep in mind his burden is light and so is his yoke.

Soon all we do is for Christ
He reigns and is in total control.
Things may look bad and challenge our faith,
but there is no one like God, our ace in the hole

We'll return to our roots and miss who we are,
God's creation, a child of the king.
There is only one way we feel right,
it's when it's praises to God that we often sing. 😌 🤍 🙏

From Aimee Cabo's *The Cure Radio Show* episode 122
"Diving into the Subconscious" #GodisTheCure

Inspired by the song "Goodbye" by Shaylen
Full video podcast: http://apple.co/2M5g2dS

3

122, #2: "Stay Next to Me" by Quinn XCII and Chelsea

Sometimes God calls us
even when we think we are not ready.
There is never a perfect time to straighten out.
It can be done one day at a time slowly and steady.

We have to abandon unhealthy ways,
distinguish between those worth keeping,
and let go of bad company,
if it is truly God we are seeking.

The more we fall in love with God,
the better we feel and the less we care
what people may think of us or who we've become
because we don't drown when coming up for air.

His word is enough, and his will does suffice,
keeping God close by our side.
Learning to love with humility
while setting aside any hatred or pride.

Seeing the good in all things that transpire
is God's grace when given our sight,
As shame and fear is removed,
when leaving the darkness as we enter God's light. 😌 🤍 🙏

From Aimee Cabo's *The Cure Radio Show* episode 122
"Diving into the Subconscious" #GodisTheCure

Inspired by the song "Stay Next To Me" by Quinn XCII and Chelsea
Full video podcast: http://apple.co/2M5g2dS

122, #1: "Amen" by King and Country

Amen, what does it mean?
God's will is always done.
He is present in every situation,
he is never changing, silent or gone.

His truth lives on,
his love is incredible, he is our boo.
The example he left us
brings us joy and makes us new.

With Jesus on our mind
in everything we think or do,
We give it our best and don't give up
because, God, it's all for you.

Simply trust our Lord.
Everything he said is tried and true.
He is our hope and dwells within
despite who we are or what we've been through.

We are never scared or alone,
with God we carry on.
We can face tomorrow because he lives, for his kingdom will come,
Thanks to Jesus, his only son. 😌 🖤 🙏

From Aimee Cabo's *The Cure Radio Show* episode 122
"Diving into the Subconscious" #GodisTheCure

Inspired by the song "Amen" by King and Country
Full video podcast: http://apple.co/2M5g2dS

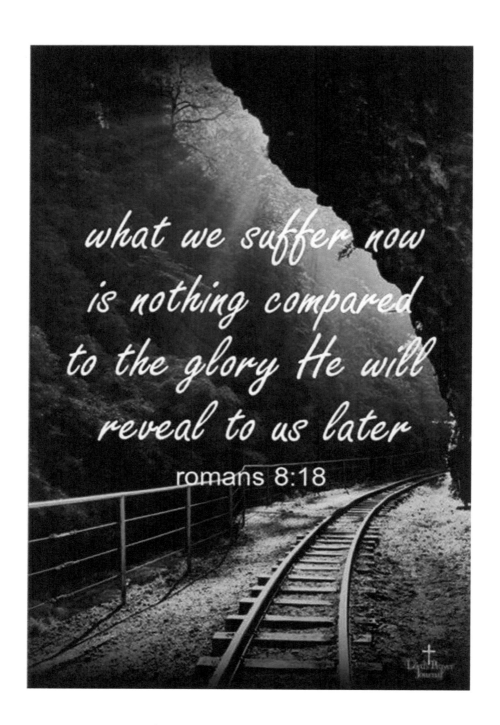

what we suffer now
is nothing compared
to the glory He will
reveal to us later

romans 8:18

121, #4: "Diamonds" by Rihanna

When we are happy,
we shine brighter than ever.
A diamond is what we can be.
With God, there isn't a storm we cannot weather.

Some of us can drown,
when treading through a raging sea
But we learn to float above.
When finding hope in God, we discover we are free.

For those who turn to God
feel the energy right away
And will then feel so alive
never to turn back or go astray.

For Jesus is the way,
and God will see us through the night,
While he provides a path to paradise
with great comfort, strength, and sight.

We will succeed and feel complete
as we illuminate so bright,
When following Jesus faithfully
in loving everyone to God's delight.

And commit to what is right
by seeking God within
So the truth can shed a light
As we learn to love the sinner, not the sin. 😌 🤍 🙏

From Aimee Cabo's *The Cure Radio Show* episode 121
"The Easy Way Out" #GodisTheCure

Inspired by the song "Diamonds" by Rihanna
Full audio podcast: http://bit.ly/3i9DmTG

The blessing
of the Lord
makes me rich

PROVERBS 10:22

121, #3: "Something Just Like This" by Chainsmokers & Coldplay

God doesn't need us to be perfect
he just wants to see us trying.
We will know right from wrong and just what to do,
when we stop falling for the lying.

We think it comes from us
without knowing how easily we are fooled,
But the enemy is real
and the influences of this world is how we are schooled.

We are not superhuman with superhero gifts
but God is all we need and surely everything to us he is
more than anything that can ever be explained.
He is in the center of our lives and our very bliss.

He made us perfect as can be,
according to his will, we were in his list.
So we can be like him
learn to love so perfectly and peacefully exist.

God watches us so tenderly
he wanted something just like this,
A love willing to die for
people he can miss.

Until we are united
he is still our greatest fan.
Look at the effort and all he's done for us
since he created us and life began. 😌 🤍 🙏

From Aimee Cabo's *The Cure Radio Show* episode 121
"The Easy Way Out" #GodisTheCure

Inspired by the song "Something Just Like This"
by Chainsmokers & Coldplay
Full video podcast: http://apple.co/2LCh0Ov

Trust in the Lord with all your heart, and lean not on your own understanding.

In all your ways acknowledge Him, and He shall direct your paths.

~ Proverbs 3:5-6

121, #2: "Monster" by Shawn Mendes and Justin Bieber

It is important to be humble
and admit the times that we were wrong.
Have a sight full of compassion,
for it is to Jesus we belong.

Failures have to happen
when experiencing success,
Otherwise it wasn't worth it,
and there is no merit nonetheless.

What's worth it won't come easy,
it seems more than we can take.
But with God nothing's impossible,
turning tragedies into miracles, simply for our sake.

There is no monster with God's children,
no matter how big or small the sin.
Forgiveness is our gift, paid in full by Jesus.
So we can do the same and find the love within. 😌 🤍 🙏

From Aimee Cabo's *The Cure Radio Show* episode 121
"The Easy Way Out" #GodisTheCure

Inspired by the song "Monster" by Shawn Mendes and Justin Bieber
Full video podcast: http://apple.co/2LCh0Ov

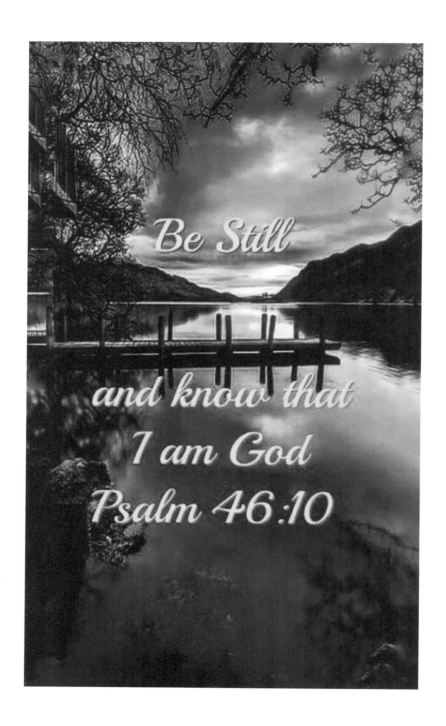

Be Still

and know that

I am God

Psalm 46:10

121, #1: "Afterglow" by Ed Sheeran

Everyday seems so amazing,
when God becomes our afterglow.
Time can change in so many ways,
full of meaning more than anyone can know.

It can be a challenge.
We face darkness here and there.
But once we come into his light,
we are not fazed by the things that seem unfair.

Our old ways that let us down
tend to fade and melt away.
It is a miracle experienced,
when growing close to God and praying every day.

When Jesus taught us how to live,
he showed us love and set us free.
Giving us hope and joy that only he provides,
beyond anything this world can offer or guarantee.

Time is precious and love is sacred,
when we truly feel alive.
By discovering our true purpose
is God's will and pleasing him is our drive.
It is through Jesus that we thrive. 😌 🤍 🙏

From Aimee Cabo's *The Cure Radio Show* episode 121
"The Easy Way Out" #GodisTheCure

Inspired by the song "Afterglow" by Ed Sheeran
Full video podcast: http://apple.co/2LCh0Ov

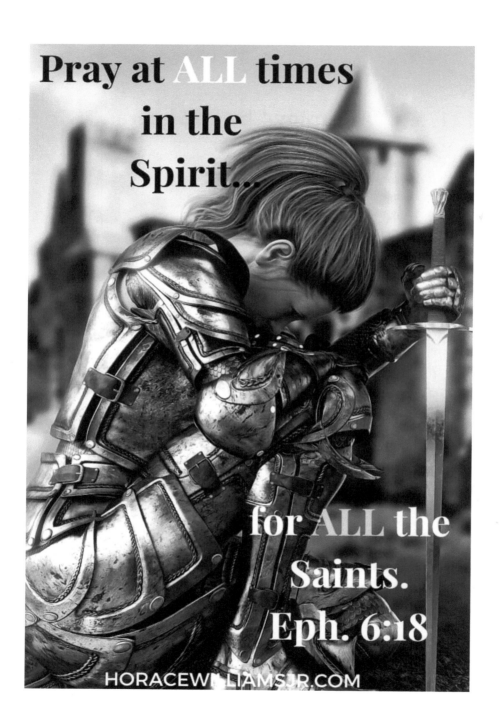

Pray at **ALL** times in the Spirit...

for **ALL** the Saints. Eph. 6:18

120, #4: "Put Your Records On" by Ritt Momney

God wants us to be ourselves,
Take it easy as we do our best.
Enjoy the moment despite the times,
weed out frustrations, he'll do the rest.

He gives us hope so we can live our dreams
and gives us sight to figure it out.
Appreciate our blessings,
walk with Christ and be devout.

We should know
Even when we're afraid,
That there
isn't a need
God has not supplied
When getting on our knees and prayed.

We live our best life
when we follow Jesus and abide.
For God's love is unconditional
and his truth trumps anything
the enemy has ever tried.
Prayer is our strength and his word the ultimate guide. 😌 🖤 🙏

From Aimee Cabo's *The Cure Radio Show* episode 120
"The Battle of Good against Evil" #GodisTheCure

Inspired by the song "Put Your Records On" by Ritt Momney,
Originally by Corinne Bailey Rae
Full video podcast: http://apple.co/38cGWZW

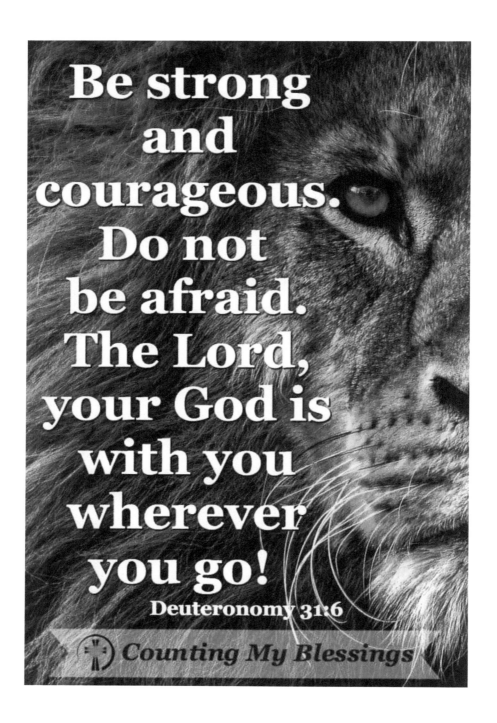

Be strong and courageous. Do not be afraid. The Lord, your God is with you wherever you go!

Deuteronomy 31:6

Counting My Blessings

120, #3: "Count On Me" by Bruno Mars

God is that true friend
we can really count on.
We are his pride and joy,
a work in progress until he is done.
He is our shining armor
when hope is gone.

He guards our sleep
and guides our days.
His love is evident
in so many ways

We are never lost
with Christ at heart,
the one we can be sure of
to play his part.

He is the God,
who is always around.
So, no matter what,
we can still be found.

His will is carefully planned,
For us and for the best.
We must trust him always
Even when it puts our faith through the test. 😌 🤍 🙏

From Aimee Cabo's *The Cure Radio Show* episode 120
"The Battle of Good against Evil" #GodisTheCure

Inspired by the song "Count On Me" by Bruno Mars
Full video podcast: http://apple.co/38cGWZW

He knows *even* the sparrows

GregOlsen.

120, #2: "Say You Won't Let Go" by James Arthur

The only way to wake up is with God
keep him in mind throughout the day.
It helps us stay on track, focus more,
and push temptations away.

With a kiss, he will send us off
and take care of every need.
So long as we pray, stay connected,
and let him take the lead.

No need to be afraid,
even in the darkest night.
He will dance us through it all
and correct us with his light.

We are beautiful to him,
we shine so bright.
When we glorify his name
in prayer and doing only what is right.

Things will always get better, rather than worse,
it is his guarantee.
When honoring his truth,
we fall in love with him to an unbelievable degree.

He loves us so, and he wants us to know
that he will stay till the end of every show.
He is our every phase, until we are old,
the one thing we don't outgrow.
His Holy Ghost will stay with us and won't let go. 😌 🤍 🙏

From Aimee Cabo's *The Cure Radio Show* episode 120
"The Battle of Good against Evil" #GodisTheCure

Inspired by the song "Say You Won't Let Go" by James Arthur
Full video podcast: http://apple.co/38cGWZW

"As far off as the sunrise is from the sunset, So far off from us he has put our transgressions." (Psalm 103:12)

120, #1: "So Done" by The Kid Laroi

This past year has been pretty challenging
pretty triumphant too.
Some of us have no idea
what great lengths some of us went through.

I am done, so done with any sinning,
big or even small.
When it came down to fighting for our families,
as we learned to run before we crawl.

Shocking as it may have been,
so many things have opened our eyes.
We are no longer numb or dumb
to what suppressed us by the enemy's disguise.
It is time we step up to the plate and rise.

God is always in control,
following him is easier said than done.
But there is no greater evil
that has conquered what God already won.

Many us who were hit
suffered great, and yet grew stronger.
For good will always win,
we are not slaves to evil any longer.

Not since Jesus conquered the world
with his life, death, and resurrection.
That saved so many souls and gave everyone direction,
saved by grace and his ultimate protection. 😌 🖤 🙏

From Aimee Cabo's *The Cure Radio Show* episode 120
"The Battle of Good against Evil" #GodisTheCure

Inspired by the song "So Done" by Kid Laroi
Full video podcast: http://apple.co/38cGWZW

HOLY FAMILY
of Nazareth

JESUS, MARY and
JOSEPH most kind,
bless us now and
in death's agony.
Protect us, keep us
in our life's journey.
Amen.

@junevreyes

119, #4: "Dance Monkey" by Tones and I

God sees us all, to him we shine.
He begs us to take his hands.
He says it is time,
For we are his and he is ours.

We know the dance, we've learned the climb.
It's more difficult, but not impossible, it's his design.
We have our gifts, he loves our style.
We are all here just for a while.

So make it even better than before,
make it count, give all you've got and even more.
And make God proud, he loves our dance.
We can rise above, given every chance

So God says move something,
just move for me.
Let's grow up, remember that he sacrificed to set us free,
so we can live up to who we are meant to be. 😌 🖤 🙏

From Aimee Cabo's *The Cure Radio Show* episode 119
"Counting Our Blessings" #GodisTheCure

Inspired by the song "Dance Monkey" by Tones and I
Full video podcast: http://apple.co/38Acs2Q

"My son, forget not my law; but let thine heart keep my commandments: For length of days, and long life, and peace, shall they add to thee."

Proverbs 3:1-2

119, #3: "Hold Me While You Wait" by Lewis Capaldi

If we open our eyes
and learn to give it more,
God will show us great things
and open yet an amazing door.

There is more to life
than having it all,
just like knowing what to do
every time we fall.

Even if we are not good enough,
God will take care of what is really tough.
Even if we feel the wait is long,
God builds us up and makes us strong.

We can always learn what is right as we wait.
God predetermined us going to heaven as our fate.
We must believe, for our faith remains
in loving Christ as we break those chains. 😌 🤍 🙏

From Aimee Cabo's *The Cure Radio Show* episode 119
"Counting Our Blessings" #GodisTheCure

Inspired by the song "Hold Me While You Wait" by Lewis Capaldi
Full video podcast: http://apple.co/38Acs2Q

JESUS

BORN AS A BABY
PREACHED AS A CHILD
KILLED AS A MAN
AROSE AS A VICTOR
COMING BACK AS A
KING

119, #2: "Holding On" by Iann Dior

God had good reasons for our existence,
he created us for love.
We know it is not for everyone,
heaven does not fit all of us just like a glove.

All of us will know God
And learn the truth,
It's a choice we are given,
Innate since our early youth.

When there is a lot to lose,
Don't be a fool for heaven's sake.

Turn to God who always tries
And does not forsake.

He will keep holding on,
he makes no mistake.
Praying, reading the Bible,
and following Jesus keeps us awake. 😌 🤍 🙏

From Aimee Cabo's *The Cure Radio Show* episode 119
"Counting Our Blessings" #GodisTheCure

Inspired by the song "Holding On" by Iann Dior
Full video podcast: http://apple.co/38Acs2Q

119, #1: "Save Your Tears" by Weeknd

Did someone break our heart?
Was it life, or did we play a part?
Who did we turn to, did we do what is right?
Or did we ignore God's plea despite our plight?

God is loving, he wants to stay,
but when we don't care, we push him away.
God dries our tears and saves them for another day.
He doesn't want us to despair or go astray.

It's a matter of trusting in him and always pray,
no matter what hits us, shocks us, or gets in the way.
The tears don't matter, when keeping faith alive,
having God not only helps us survive but also thrive.

Sad moments always come and go,
it is just a tool provided that will help us grow.
It will not steal our courage or destroy our joy
because we are never the enemy's toy.

In life God matters,
and we should show that we care,
for when we do,
there isn't anything in life we cannot bear. 😌 🖤 🙏

From Aimee Cabo's *The Cure Radio Show* episode 119
"Counting Our Blessings" #GodisTheCure

Inspired by the song "Save Your Tears" by Weeknd
Full video podcast: http://apple.co/38Acs2Q

You may see all my
weaknesses

But look closer
For I have a

Lion

living within me
who is Christ Jesus

118, #4: "Intentions" by Justin Bieber

You can be perfect,
be like me, is what God said.
Follow me, you are my image,
I am the life and the bread.

I created you with great intention,
to every detail I gave careful attention.

All was planned –
the good times and the sad.
It made us grow,
even though at times it made us mad.

It takes some time
creating a masterpiece.
It can be difficult and confusing,
but how else must faith eventually increase.

We can truly be an asset
when showered by his grace.
So kiss the ring, God's our king,
and we are his base. 😌 🖤 🙏

From Aimee Cabo's *The Cure Radio Show* episode 118
"Finding Faith Within" #GodisTheCure

Inspired by the song "Intentions" by Justin Bieber
Full video podcast: http://apple.co/3pdcxQF

118, #3: "Hawái" by Maluma & The Weekend

Tell me, what is your heaven?
The things we think that make us happy or we need.
We are lying to ourselves if we think it's in this world.
Only family, our love for others, and those who believe in us can plant that seed.

It started with our heavenly father.
who opens up our mind.
He presents it at the perfect time,
for so long we didn't even know
we were so blind.

But how would you like to be on vacation,
free from drinking, smoking, vaping, or any other frustration?

When we need nothing at all,
it is God that is in the center of our lives,
Where we may trip and stumble, but never fall.

It's no longer an everyday war we must fight
but a greater understanding of what is truly right.
There is no greater feeling than being free.
Only God is that constant.
For in this life, every day is a blessing, and there's no guarantee.

Finding purpose through Christ is the greatest way to be.
It's what allows us to find meaning in all the beauty we see.
God provides the true path for us all,
for which he willingly sacrificed himself, taking the fall.

God provides the grace
that will surely make us tough.
As his children, we are treasured and he is all we need,
when God's love becomes enough. 😌 🤍 🙏

From Aimee Cabo's *The Cure Radio Show* episode 118
"Finding Faith Within" #GodisTheCure

Inspired by the song "Hawái" by Maluma and The Weekend
Full video podcast: http://apple.co/3pdcxQF

35

In
God's Grace
each dawn is a gift
and every day a miracle...

To every thing
there is a season,
and a time to every purpose
under the heaven.

ECCLESIASTES 3:1

36

118, #2: "Be Like That"
by Swae Lee & Khalid

When I hear this song, what echoes most is
"It hurts sometimes to be like that,"
Especially the things
that make us fall on our face flat.

Crazy things not experienced before,
Is it possible that we could endure anymore?
Wondering what is going on.
We are never ourselves with our true sense gone.

We always need God back,
It will always be like that.
Only God can keep us sane,
In a world that can be too much,
Otherwise it becomes a drain.
And we just learn to live in vain.

We know what we shouldn't do
and who is really a friend.
We are not better on our own,
there is no reason to pretend.

God can give us everything if we only turn to him,
he'll keep us warm and full of love.
All we have to do is follow through,
And just comply with God above.

In his word we must abide,
For his ways are humble,
never full of pride.
It doesn't seem right if it's from God
we feel we have to constantly hide. 😌 🤍 🙏

From Aimee Cabo's *The Cure Radio Show* episode 118
"Finding Faith Within" #GodisTheCure

Inspired by the song "Be Like That" by Swaelee and Hegreatkhalid
Full video podcast: http://apple.co/3pdcxQF

The Best **Decision** I ever made was to follow Jesus Christ.

©GodFruits.com

118, #1: "Fix You" by Coldplay

When will we try to reach our greatest potential?
What will it take for us to acknowledge our best?
Will it be time to let go and let God guide us,
so we can finally learn that in God we can rest?

Life can be scary, there are moments that will drop us to our knees,
but it is our hearts, beautiful soul, and our potential that God always sees.
Though is there a better position to be in to pray?
When we hit rock bottom, it really is the only way.

These times have been dark,
but his light will always shine
above all the noise, for there is nothing
like God's sweet love, so divine.

We can only fool ourselves for so long,
believe the hype as we falsely carry on.

It's worth giving God a try.
It's with him that we learn,
grow wings, and start to fly.

There is so much that we can discover,
otherwise we will never know
how much there is to recover.
Only freedom through Christ can fix you,
create confidence and peace like no other. 😌 🤍 🙏

From Aimee Cabo's *The Cure Radio Show* episode 118
"Finding Faith Within" #GodisTheCure

Inspired by the song "Fix You" by Coldplay
Full video podcast: http://apple.co/3pdcxQF

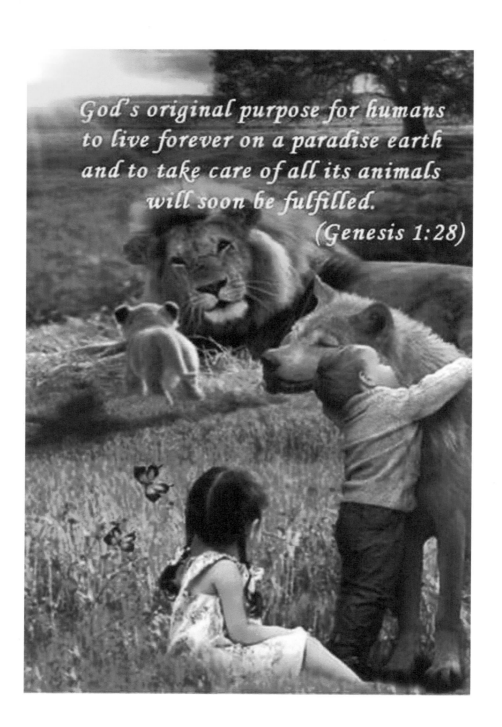

God's original purpose for humans to live forever on a paradise earth and to take care of all its animals will soon be fulfilled. *(Genesis 1:28)*

117, #4: "Keeping It Real" by Shaggy

When we were young, it seemed a whole lot easier.
We didn't care so much, as everything looked so much prettier.
Then life can happen and truly hit us hard,
Making us wonder what is this that left us scarred.

But in our pain and through our struggle,
We find reasons to continue, though we may still be in trouble.

If we dwell upon the sorrow,
There is always someone suffering worse.
As long as we are alive,
there is hope every tomorrow.

Doesn't matter if we feel blue,
We can turn to God and those in heaven,
There is no better crew.

Feeling blessed is how we keep it real
And reimagine how we feel.

Gratitude and serving others
Is how we take the focus off ourselves.
And learn to truly care for one another,

Only God can make this happen.

Once we have tried it all,
We see it is God who is always there,
When answering his call.

To catch us every turn,
And show us there is hope,
When there is a lesson, we must learn

And it is a blessing in disguise,
When we trust God's word
over Satan's lies. 😌 🖤 🙏

From Aimee Cabo's *The Cure Radio Show* episode 117
"Are We Our Brother's Keeper" #GodisTheCure

Inspired by the song "Keeping It Real" by Shaggy
Full video podcast: https://apple.co/3mdn7Fh

WE KNOW WHAT REAL LOVE IS BECAUSE

Jesus gave up his life.

FOR US.

1 JOHN 3:16

117, #3: "The One You Need" by Bret Eldredge

Only once a year,
winter comes and it gets cold outside.
Though there can be many seasons
where we feel bad inside.

Finding little comfort
and feeling as if there is nowhere we can easily hide,
God is with us, ever vigilant, caring for us unrelenting,
even when hope seems dim from all the tears we've cried

The world and those we trust can also hurt us,
should remind us of how Jesus took the cross.
Sharing the pain just brings us nearer.
Getting closer to Jesus makes our vision clearer.

He wants to hold us so very tight.
We can rest assure that all our worries
we can give to God, who always wins the fight

No one loves us more than our creator.
We must invite him and let him in,
For he provides all that we need,
In order to survive and feel peace within.

Who is ever constant, he wants us to know
that we can rest in him,
and we will discover things unheard of, more to life
than can be imagined, for his love does overflow. 😌 🖤 🙏

From Aimee Cabo's *The Cure Radio Show* episode 117
"Are We Our Brother's Keeper" #GodisTheCure

Inspired by the song "The One You Need" by Bret Eldredge
Full video podcast: https://apple.co/3mdn7Fh

Humans
will not be the only
ones to benefit from
the peaceful world
God will soon bring.

"For we know that
all creation keeps on
groaning together
and being in pain
together until now."
(Romans 8:22)

117, #2: "Going Out" by Role Model

We have all been there
Where we don't feel our best.
It is better that no one realizes it.
We like to blend in like the rest.

When the moods are unpredictable,
frustration can set in.
Taking all the loses as they come,
we don't care to win.

If we lose our faith,
it can quickly grow progressive.
But when God turns suffering into strength,
it turns out quite impressive.

We are given a specific purpose
integrated with a cross.
It is what unites us to our heavenly father,
who took the greatest loss.

When we accept our fate
And learn to suffer well,
there is no longer an impediment
for how we should excel.

If it wasn't for the Lord's great love,
we would all be lost to the glory and the promises
given to us from above. 😌 🤍 🙏

From Aimee Cabo's *The Cure Radio Show* episode 117
"Are We Our Brother's Keeper" #GodisTheCure

Inspired by the song "Going Out" by Role Model
Full video podcast: https://apple.co/3mdn7Fh

The sun is a daily reminder that we too can rise from the darkness...

"...Although I dwell in the darkness, Jehovah will be my light." (Micah 7:8)

117, #1: "Chandelier" by Sia

We remember many times being a mess,
Feeling a failure and even much less.

But we got really good, despite any shame,
In denying it all, including the pain.
And just keep moving on,
For there was much more we thought we could gain.

Ignoring the hurt and believing the best,
regardless of what had transpired, we put it to rest.
There was no room for the sorrow,
drowning with lies like there was no tomorrow.

Holding back any tears,
how did we get by all these years?
Drinking kept our glass full
Until God showed us the light,
Embraced by his love,
We surrendered to our sweet delight.

With God, there is a much better way,
in life some of us have a heavy price we must pay.

We can swing from the chandelier,
but how much longer can we afford to be cavalier?

Jesus knew this too well,
on the cross he provided us freedom,
for which we can start over, it is never farewell.

Instead of holding on to dear life
and living on edge with a two-sided knife,
we can turn to God who sees our true best.
Sometimes in life, it is merely a test.

But with God, we are never apart,
For he is deep within every heart.
To truly feel peace, faith is what it will take.
All can be mended when living life and giving it all for his sake. 😌 🤍 🙏

From Aimee Cabo's *The Cure Radio Show* episode 117
"Are We Our Brother's Keeper" #GodisTheCure

Inspired by the song "Chandelier" by Sia
Full video podcast: https://apple.co/3mdn7Fh

Paradise earth...
truly a thrilling
hope for
the future!

"The righteous will possess the earth,
And they will live forever on it."
(Psalm 37:29)

116, #4: "Bummerland" by Ajr

It is a bummer, where have we arrived,
where is the love.
Our ideas of life and everything we believed in
from our heavenly father above.

If we have been hit hard before,
think again, it can always get worse.
It can get us derailed,
but please stay on course.

Know that with God,
there is only one way
that is up, we must pray,
God never goes away.

Trust in God's plan,
Though we may not understand.
Just know that his love for us is greater,
Than every grain of sand.
It is with God that we see beauty
And we learn to take a stand. 😌 🤍 🙏

From Aimee Cabo's *The Cure Radio Show* episode 116
"From Victim to Victor" #GodisTheCure

Inspired by the song "Bummerland" by Ajr
Full video podcast: https://apple.co/3qyJGHU

Not all hearts are the same... the heart of one who loves and trusts Jehovah is totally different...

"He will not fear bad news. His heart is steadfast, trusting in Jehovah. His heart is unshakable; he is not afraid;" (Psalm 112:7,8)

116, #3: "Fallin, Why Don't We" by Ajr

There comes a moment that some of us
are left with nothing but God and I.
It seems unfortunate, feeling alone,
but there is more than meets the eye.

It is when we don't question
as God reaches out the most,
Despite what we're suffering or how we self-diagnose,
we cannot ignore the Holy Ghost.

We can feel reckless
but can't stop our hearts from beating.
Having God present
is like no other feeling.

How far will we jump,
to God we give in,
Do we prefer peace within,
or will we succumb to sin?

We can keep falling,
as long as God is our muse,
Despite the outcome unknown,
who will we choose?

What do I have to give up, Lord,
what should I do?
When it comes to you, God, I don't care what I go through.
Anything I do, let it be inspired only from you. 😌 🤍 🙏

From Aimee Cabo's *The Cure Radio Show* episode 116
"From Victim to Victor" #GodisTheCure

Inspired by the song "Fallin, Why Don't We" by Ajr
Full video podcast: https://apple.co/3qyJGHU

Soon, faithful humans will enjoy life to the full in the upcoming Paradise

(Isaiah 65:17)

116, #2: "Sober Up" by Ajr

When we decide to follow Jesus,
we straighten our life.
As loyal as we may be, even long-term friendships
can bring about strife.

It seemed fun while it lasted,
we were fooled for a while,
But how did we feel without God,
every time we were faced with a trial?

We can grow faster than others,
it is not leaving them behind.
We can pray for them and correct our ways,
but we can no longer be blind.

We know peace, since we are made in Christ's image,
how is it again?
Being sober and growing up,
not even fazed by the rain.

The days we feel happy
no matter what is going on,
Is when we paint with our favorite color and are young once again,
once God's will is done. 😌 🤍 🙏

From Aimee Cabo's *The Cure Radio Show* episode 116
"From Victim to Victor" #GodisTheCure

Inspired by the song "Sober Up" by Ajr
Full video podcast: https://apple.co/3qyJGHU

There's nothing more dangerous to our personal future than a closed mind that denies spiritual realities...

"Keep your minds fixed on the things above, not on the things on the earth." (Colossians 3:2)

116, #1: "Overrwhelmed" by Royal & The Serpent

So many things can shock us all at once,
Making us feel overwhelmed and needing space.
Who can help when it hits you from all directions?
If not for God's unconditional love and grace.

It is God's most precious children,
The enemy loves to attack.
So we can question ourselves, believe we are broken,
Like there is no way out and there is no turning back.

When we become someone
We don't recognize,
Insecurity and fear kicks in,
And it is ourselves we despise.

The enemy is clever
And takes advantage of bad situations.
But God is bigger
And lets us know it is simply temptations.

God will provide all that we need
And open our eyes,
For our heavenly father
Is never mute to our cries. 😌 🤍 🙏

From Aimee Cabo's *The Cure Radio Show* episode 116
"From Victim to Victor" #GodisTheCure

Inspired by the song "Overwhelmed" by Royal & Serpent
Full video podcast: https://apple.co/3qyJGHU

Jeremiah 33:3

Call to me and I will answer you and show you great and unsearchable things you do not know.

115, #4: "Love Bug" by Jonas Brothers

I am speechless.
I thought I knew love.
That is until I got to really know
Our heavenly father from above.

I can still struggle every day
And live on the edge,
But it is still amazing,
Loving God is my solemn pledge.

Speechless I am also
When things go wrong,
Grateful always that because of God
I have remained strong.

I was hit with the greatest
love bug around,
when God showed me the world
from the day I was found.

I only felt complete when discovering
That the missing part of me
Was the one who created us,
Sacrificed his life to redeem us,
and set us free. 😌 🖤 🙏

From Aimee Cabo's *The Cure Radio Show* episode 115
"Establishing Good Relationships" #GodisTheCure

Inspired by the song "Love Bug" by Jonas Brothers
Full video podcast: https://apple.co/3l4Ugml

115, #3: "I'm Yours" by Jason Mraz

There are times we try to figure it out
only to discover our humanity,
It can put into perspective
our deceptions and our vanity.

If pleasing God is what we aim to do,
we will succeed, never fail, it is our virtue.
Provided to us all, but practiced by the few.

God says,
I am yours and we are his,
it isn't complicated,
it is heaven's kiss.

It is our fate,
let's open our eyes
and be set free,
the future no one can foresee.

Don't compromise yourself
or believe the lies,
for God,
there is no limit to the skies.
Once with God,
his children prosper and always rise. 😌 🖤 🙏

From Aimee Cabo's *The Cure Radio Show* episode 115
"Establishing Good Relationships" #GodisTheCure

Inspired by the song "I'm Yours" by Jason Mraz
Full video podcast: https://apple.co/3l4Ugml

115, #2: "Como La Flor" by Selena

Heartbreaks come in many forms.
We know it hurts and its full of pain.
Nonetheless we carry on and wish the best for everyone,
Sometimes it is shocking and can drive one insane.

Hopefully, we learn
where we went wrong
and if there is someone else
to whom we might belong.

But know that change starts with me.
I must become who I want the other person to be.

There are people worth fighting for,
and there is reason to increase our effort and do more.

Love must be nurtured
In order to grow,
Just like a flower, God showed us love and kindness
From the first hello. 😊 🖤 🙏

From Aimee Cabo's *The Cure Radio Show* episode 115
"Establishing Good Relationships" #GodisTheCure

Inspired by the song "Como La Flor" by Selena
Full video podcast: https://apple.co/3l4Ugml

115, #1: "Go Crazy" by Chris Brown and Young Thug

When we ask God to grow,
it can sometimes rain.
It can have us up all night,
but rest assured, it's never in vain.

When life hits hard, we miss God,
the one who takes our battles and makes things right.
We are mistaken if we believe that, alone,
we can win the fight.

We are reminded, God is all we need,
as discouraging as it may be,
Only he can clear our minds, bring us peace,
change our lives, and set us free.

God knows our heart and when we are falling apart.
He can tell if we are being real.
And the more genuine we become,
the greater our love skill and the more pain we feel.

With God, what we do is amazing,
he is telling us just go crazy,
he will believe in us
even when our eyesight goes hazy.

Blind trust builds faith
as we become our best.
There will be times that we feel weary,
just know that God provides rest. 😌 🖤 🙏

From Aimee Cabo's *The Cure Radio Show* episode 115
"Establishing Good Relationships" #GodisTheCure

Inspired by the song "Go Crazy" by Chris Brown And Young Thug
Full video podcast: https://apple.co/3l4Ugml

"He that is without sin among you,
let him first cast a stone at her."

John 8:7 (KJV)

114, #4: "Know Your Worth" by Khalid and Disclosure

Do we know our worth,
Is our existence a mistake?
It was God who is omnipotent
Who sent his only son to sacrifice his life,
Despite heaven's cry, only for our sake.

By sin, we cannot be bound.
Thanks to Jesus, it is possible to be found.

Just look around, who is the one who puts us first,
Redeems us when we are truly sorry and overlooks the worst?

Don't believe the lies, it is not all in your head,
Don't lose hope and embrace God's word instead.

We can always keep our head up as long as we're alive.
Remember that, with God, despite the pain, all survivors thrive. 😌 🤍 🙏

From Aimee Cabo's *The Cure Radio Show* episode 114
"Women Who Defy The Odds" #GodisTheCure

Inspired by the song "Know Your Worth" by Khalid And Disclosure
Full video podcast: https://apple.co/3f3lSqe

From the minute they first met, their lives would change forever...

Zen to Zany

114, #3: "Beautiful Crazy" by Luke Combs

Unconditional love means
The person you love is amazing,
There is no wrong they can do,
Just mistakes and lessons awaiting.

Only the best side we see and the good times
Is what we are always embracing.

Forgiving is easy because
Of the way that she dances.
It can be tough,
But it is worth taking chances.

The heart is what matters,
When it is in the right place.
Any challenge or duration is irrelevant when love is patient,
And we walk in God's grace. 😌 🤍 🙏

From Aimee Cabo's *The Cure Radio Show* episode 114
"Women Who Defy The Odds" #GodisTheCure

Inspired by the song "Beautiful Crazy" by Luke Combs
Full video podcast: https://apple.co/3f3lSqe

And the Word became
flesh and dwelt
among us,
and we beheld His glory,
the glory as
of the only
begotten of the
Father full of
grace and truth
-John 1:14

114, #2: "Old Me" by 5seconds of Summer

Life has its highs and lows,
Sometimes it feels as if we are constantly taking the blows.
Training it must be,
Or there must be
something holding us back from being free.

Is getting by just enough?
How many times do we need to play the role of being tough?

Some of us don't believe in giving up,
And we realize we have been wrong.
We learned too from it, made the best out of it,
And made our faith strong.

To the enemy… we can shut the door
And acknowledge we need to do more.

The lessons we learned from the past and our mistakes
Were a small price to pay,
If it brings us closer to God
When we are brought to our knees and pray.

The world can never slow us,
despite the knocking on the door.
God is love and the truth, we are his,
and it is God who we adore. 😌 🤍 🙏

From Aimee Cabo's *The Cure Radio Show* episode 114
"Women Who Defy The Odds" #GodisTheCure

Inspired by the song "Old Me" by 5 Seconds of Summer
Full video podcast: https://apple.co/3f3lSqe

114, #1: "Where Is The Love" by Black Eyed Peas

We can sometimes feel strange when life suddenly changes,
And it seems that down is up and up is down.
Where we once felt secure,
Now we struggle to smile instead of frown.

If peace and love should prevail
How is it that there are days that are difficult to exhale?

Have we compromised our values,
Taken the easier route, and settled for less?
Or are we willing to suffer with devotion to God,
Move forward and profess love, nonetheless?

It was shocking how eyes were open,
But we still focus on love
Just because we are God's children,
And we receive instructions from above.

More than words
We need to walk the walk.
Follow Jesus always, for when life has us discouraged,
Only God removes that block.

Father, father, help us, we've been humbled
and find there is only hope in you.
Where is the love? We ask ourselves, confident you'll provide it
and grateful that our faith will get us through. 😌 🤍 🙏

From Aimee Cabo's *The Cure Radio Show* episode 114
"Women Who Defy The Odds" #GodisTheCure

Inspired by the song "Where Is The Love" by Black Eyed Peas
Full video podcast: https://apple.co/3f3lSqe

Forgive those who have harmed you, not because they deserve it, but because you do.

Forgive yourself for holding on to resentment for so long and depriving yourself of inner peace, tranquility and happiness.

www.PurposeFairy.com

113, #4: "I Love You Baby" by Illy and Emilee

I hear those words, "I love you baby," and it melts my heart.
I hear it from the one that makes things right…
The one I know I can truly depend on,
trust and need in this constant fight.

God can replace the loneliness
we feel at night.
Trust him when he says he will provide,
show us the way… even in darkness, we will see light.

It is his love
that keeps us going,
because of Jesus and his sacrifice,
this movement keeps on growing.

Ever wonder why some of us walk around
unafraid and glowing?
Even when it is not expected, once we follow him,
his love for us is truly showing.

Because it is God's providence
that has taken place,
and through his mercy, we conquer all,
when we demonstrate his grace. 😌 🖤 🙏

From Aimee Cabo's *The Cure Radio Show* episode 113
"Cyberbullying And Crime" #GodisTheCure

Inspired by the song "I Love You Baby" by Llly And Emilee
Full video podcast: https://apple.co/38pXYUT

113, #3: "Take You Dancing" by Jason Derulo

I can imagine God telling us…
Let me take you dancing.
There is so much he can show us, even more that we can imagine.
We just need to do our best moves.

We must believe,
Despite the pain,
Remove all doubt, let faith see us through,
When we are against the grain.

We will conquer every challenge.
With resolve and every tear,
It was God who said we shouldn't fear,
As long as we keep him near.

Ever since we were created,
God knew that we could do it.
It's a dance floor like no other
If we listen to his asking,
It's a lovely rhythm known to many who found peace,
Two-stepping to our father. 😌 🖤 🙏

From Aimee Cabo's *The Cure Radio Show* episode 113
"Cyberbullying And Crime" #GodisTheCure

Inspired by the song "Take You Dancing" by Jason Derulo
Full video podcast: https://apple.co/38pXYUT

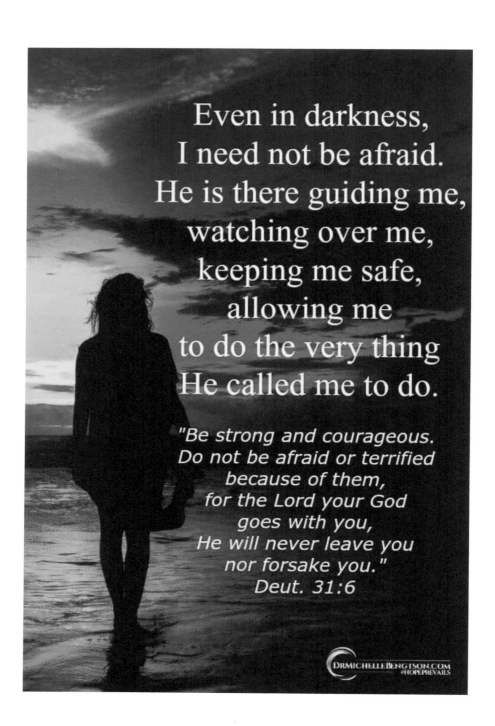

Even in darkness,
I need not be afraid.
He is there guiding me,
watching over me,
keeping me safe,
allowing me
to do the very thing
He called me to do.

*"Be strong and courageous.
Do not be afraid or terrified
because of them,
for the Lord your God
goes with you,
He will never leave you
nor forsake you."
Deut. 31:6*

DRMICHELLEBENGTSON.COM
#HOPEPREVAILS

113, #2: "Cardigan" by Taylor Swift

We step into the train of life.
Deep down inside we all know Christ.
It can be hard terrain…
Blood, sweat, tears, and those things that leave a stain.

Nonetheless we muster through.
There's a greater calling we must attend to…
Whether we are aware of it or not, it is available for all.
We either rise to the occasion, or we are determined to fall.

No one knows their time.
What has been given, can be taken away from the divine.
He holds the keys to heaven's gate,
And he allowed us free will to choose our fate.

Only God knows the ending, and he will linger around endlessly,
Hang with us even when we curse him,
Because he knew once the thrill was gone,
It doesn't matter what we know or even if we are young,
we will come back to him. Ultimately, it is God's will that's done. 😌 🤍 🙏

From Aimee Cabo's *The Cure Radio Show* episode 113
"Cyberbullying And Crime" #GodisTheCure

Inspired by the song "Cardigan" by Taylor Swift
Full video podcast: https://apple.co/38pXYUT

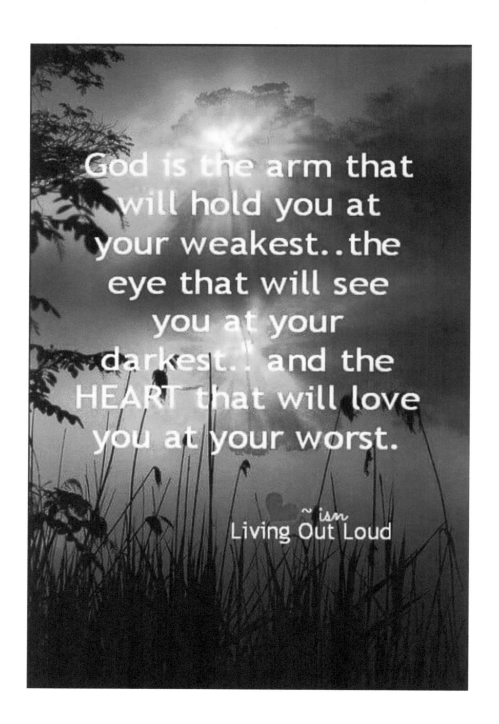

God is the arm that will hold you at your weakest..the eye that will see you at your darkest.. and the HEART that will love you at your worst.

~ ism
Living Out Loud

113, #1: "Wonder" by Shawn Mendes

Sometimes we wonder what it is like to be loved
When we lose our faith and start to feel low.

We can be so hard on ourselves when we believe the lies,
Feeling like there is no one to turn to and nowhere to go.

We feel so very small,
When we read about the saints,
Believing it is too difficult and it can never be us at all,
Despite the fact that it's our call.

The crying never ends
When this world conditions us to search for outlets
In the wrong places, where there are no friends.

Still we wonder, as we close our eyes,
What it takes to have God truly on our side.
Dreaming of a day when everyone feels it,
Despite all the tears they've cried. 😌 🖤 🙏

From Aimee Cabo's *The Cure Radio Show* episode 113
"Cyberbullying And Crime" #GodisTheCure

Inspired by the song "Wonder" by Shawn Mendes
Full video podcast: https://apple.co/38pXYUT

112, #4: "Trust In You" by Lauren Diegle

Trusting God
is required for peace.
We can try every avenue but to no avail.
Just remember we are God's masterpiece.

Dreams can be shattered,
and we must confess,
there is no winning without God,
there is no success.

He is our king, a mighty warrior,
loving father, who will take the fight.
Anything we go through,
he will make just right.

Oftentimes we cry out to you, when our faith is under fire,
leaving us no clue.
Nonetheless, God, we trust in you, you're the God who stays,
loves us greatly, and will see us through.

There will be a time that we come to see
That we must treasure forgiveness for it sets us free,
and our two favorite sayings will be:
God I am sorry and you are so good to me. 😌 🤍 🙏

Inspired by the song "Trust In You" by Lauren Diegle
Full video podcast: https://apple.co/2HZvN42

"FOR I WILL RESTORE
HEALTH TO YOU AND
HEAL YOU OF YOUR WOUNDS"
says the Lord.

Jeremiah 30:17

112, #3: "Hold On" by Chord Overstreet

For some of us, it can be a treacherous endless highway,
And when it hurts the most, God seems silent, but he is with us.

Despite life's challenges, we can depend on God,
We are merely humans, he is the one we know we can trust.

When there is a shock, all we can do is increase in prayer.
We could feel weak as if we are living a nightmare,
But stay close to God
For he will never allow anything we cannot bear.

A broken heart can hit very hard,
Leaving one feeling truly scarred.
We never want to let go of those we love,
But there is no need to understand God's mercy from above.

Let God carry us through and make it right,
It is his battle and not our fight. 😌 🤍 🙏

From Aimee Cabo's *The Cure Radio Show* episode 112
"When Faith Is Challenged" #GodisTheCure

Inspired by the song "Hold On" by Chord Overstreet
Full video podcast: https://apple.co/2HZvN42

112, #2: "Lonely" by Justin Bieber and Benny Blanco

It can be a very lonely place to have to do it all,
Yet feel alone and misunderstood.
The enemy can play his games, get us to question ourselves,
Even what we believe and he implants every falsehood.

The toughest battles are given to God's strongest soldiers.
Suffering comes in waves, and it may never calm down.

When there is a lesson learned, to God, we only get closer.

That is how we learn to love the cross and remember God's crown.

I like to pray that I have eyes to see,
With God's sight,
Even though it may be killing me.

He always shows me the light.

There will be times we fall,
Feeling that no one is listening and there is no hope at all.
Listen carefully, it is gentle, when there is no one to turn to,
Try receiving God's call.

He was there with us all along.
When we suffered, guess who made us strong.
The enemy could be stringing us along,
but it will pass, and he will not succeed,
When it's God to whom we belong. 😊 🤍 🙏

From Aimee Cabo's *The Cure Radio Show* episode 112
"When Faith Is Challenged" #GodisTheCure

Inspired by the song "Lonely" by Justin Bieber and Benny Blanco
Full video podcast: https://apple.co/2HZvN42

112, #1: "Golden" by Harry Styles and Adam Levine

God's love for us is unbelievable, to him we are golden.
He wants to open our eyes.
Sometimes we tend to lose focus
When we are believing the enemy's lies.

But God takes us back to the light,
Truly making us bright
So we can do what is right.

He gives us needed strength when we feel hopeless,
For the enemy wants us to believe we are broken.
He will take advantage of tough situations,
Until it is God that has spoken.
It will be scary, so faith can increase,
And there will be times that hearts get broken.

The hardest thing to face is being alone,
And it can feel that way.
When life hits you hard, one's faith is challenged.
That is when it's most important to pray.

As long as God loves us,
We are golden.
And when faith survives it all,
We realize we are chosen. 😌 🤍 🙏

From Aimee Cabo's *The Cure Radio Show* episode 112
"When Faith Is Challenged" #GodisTheCure

Inspired by the song "Golden" by Harry Styles and Adam Levine
Full video podcast: https://apple.co/2HZvN42

111, #4: "Haunt You" by X-Lovers and Chloe Moriondo

God has loved us
From the very first time,
And when he died for us,
He proved compassion that is divine.

We cannot imagine
One day without him by our side,
And he will never let go,
So many times for us he cried.

Now we have his ghost always with us,
Seeing every move we make
We cannot fool him or hide,
There are notes that he will take.

He is never part-time.
When we are behaving bad,
He cries even more,
And without him, we are sad.

If I am ruled by the things of this world
Of which I detest most is pride,
I can never move forward,
And I'll be dying inside.

God wants no one else to have you because we are his,
And we can only find peace
When its God we pursue, as our faith will increase
And God's grace will release. 😌 🤍 🙏

From Aimee Cabo's *The Cure Radio Show* episode 112
"Faith Under Fire" #GodisTheCure

Inspired by the song "Haunt You" by X-Lovers
Full video podcast: https://apple.co/3kIp2C9

89

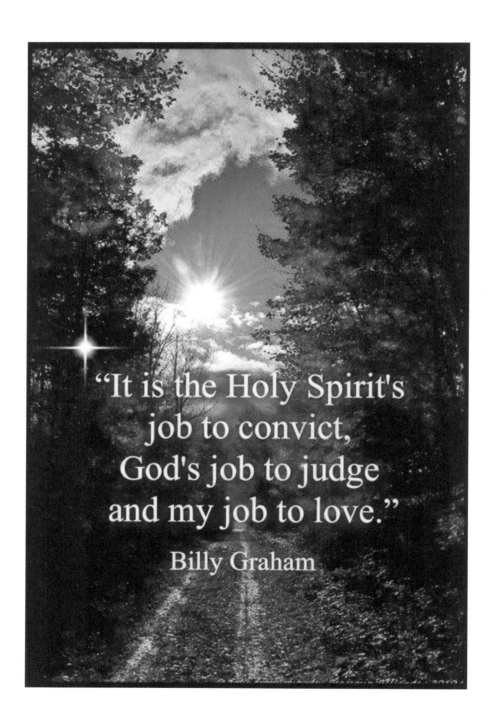

"It is the Holy Spirit's
job to convict,
God's job to judge
and my job to love."

Billy Graham

111, #3: "Nobody But You" by Blake Shelton

Looking back,
I realize there was a time I wasted,
But it was all for a reason,
Some of which I didn't get and sometimes I was tested.

Don't care who to blame, I have no regrets,
I can never be the same.
I had to choose the truth
Or continue playing Satan's game.

There is only one thing I know,
I can never live without.
There was only one God that never gave up,
Even when he should have, as I was feeling doubt.

The heart can get pretty heavy when we take the easy road,
But remember, there's a better choice to make.
Eventually we die, and when we do,
What path do we take? 😔 🤍 🙏

From Aimee Cabo's *The Cure Radio Show* episode 112
"Faith Under Fire" #GodisTheCure

Inspired by the song "Nobody But You" by Blake Shelton
Full video podcast: https://apple.co/3kIp2C9

Nothing feels bettter
than knowing
God loves you,

that He is always
there for you,
and that He will always
take care of you.

111, #2: "Levitating" by Dua Lipa

God knows we belong to him,
He created us with care.
He left a holy book for us to read
That we can take with us anywhere,
In hopes we prosper in life
And never surrender to despair.

Regardless of who we are,
It is never too late to do what's right,
Even if we've gone too far.

It is an amazing feeling knowing God.
Challenges happen, and they bother us,
Especially if its unjust, but God brings good from it
And there is a lesson learned when it is God we trust.

God's love for us will last forever, rain or shine. It is never better.
Amidst the dark, everyone can be a light,
and every night God will certainly take the fight.
We are his sugar boo.
Don't we levitate when we experience miracles
and realize how we survived all that we been through?

He can be our moonlight, dance with us, be our starlight,
we can fly with him with renewed sight.
This ride is endless if we live God's way,
if we put him first, and we obey.
We will never go dark, regress, or go astray. 😌 🖤 🙏

From Aimee Cabo's *The Cure Radio Show* episode 112
"Faith Under Fire" #GodisTheCure

Inspired by the song "Levitating" by Dua Lipa
Full video podcast: https://apple.co/3kIp2C9

111, #1: "Stereo Hearts" by Gym Class Heroes and Adam Levine

I can imagine God being my stereo.
His heart always beats for us.
All we need to do is listen and follow through,
especially in times that seem the toughest.
That's when faith counts more in all you do.

Tune up your prayer life,
especially when feeling your low.
It's when we are the closest.
that we are most attacked by our greatest foe.

This melody God meant for us, yes.
It's more difficult to sing along,
but God will never do us wrong.
It can be a harder road for some,
but it's the only peace we'll find that's worth it
because of who we can become.

Do we take God seriously, proudly think of him and speak of him,
like a boombox that you would turn up?
Trust him blindly despite any fear,
believe the impossible,
knowing that God provides and he is always near.

Sometimes things don't go the way we would like them to,
or even within the timeframe we expect.
Please don't get mad, there's no reason to project.
We should never shift the blame,
only God has perfect timing, and only God removes the shame.

But if we finally find our note,
God can take us by the hand,
show us more than we can imagine
and provide any strength needed on demand.

Keep him close, always on your mind,
speak to him quite often, for God is truly kind.
If we live by his word intently shortly, we will find,
there's a solution every time.
God's love for us is endless and his plan perfectly divine. 😌 🤍 🙏

From Aimee Cabo's *The Cure Radio Show* episode 112 "Faith Under Fire" #GodisTheCure

Inspired by the song "Stereo Hearts" by Gym Class Heroes and Adam Levine
Full video podcast: https://apple.co/3kIp2C9